The Encyclopedia of Blues Chords

Wise Publications
London/New York/Paris/Sydney/Copenhagen/Madrid

Exclusive Distributors:
Music Sales Limited
14-15 Berners Street,
London W1T 3LJ, UK.
Music Sales Corporation
257 Park Avenue South,
New York, NY 10010, USA.
Music Sales Pty Limited
20 Resolution Drive, Caringbah,
NSW 2229, Australia.

Order No. AM92592
ISBN 0-7119-4669-8
This book © Copyright 1997 by Wise Publications

Unauthorised reproduction of any part of this publication by any
means including photocopying is an infringement of copyright.

Cover design by Studio Twenty, London
Compiled and edited by Jack Long
Music processed by Woodrow Edition

Introductory Notes

1. The chords in this book are voiced in a way that makes them easy to find and play effectively. But that doesn't mean you can't play them differently if you want to.

   The notes contained in the right hand can be rearranged in any order you like, and will still represent the chord symbol shown, like this:

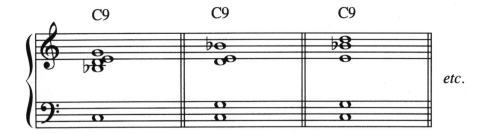

etc.

   The left hand can also be changed to alter the chord structure. Sometimes, when this is specifically required, the left hand alteration will be indicated by a 'cut' (or 'slash') chord, consisting of a chord symbol followed by a sloping line (the 'cut' or 'slash'), followed by the root, or bass note, that you need to play. C/E, for instance, means that a chord of C is to be played with an E root, or bass note.

   Here's one way of playing that:

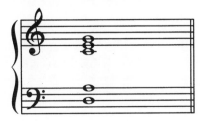

   In addition you will often see 'cut' chords containing a root not found in the chord itself. Am7/D, for instance, played like this:

   is actually D11, described in a more commonly understood fashion for those who may not know what D11 means. Now, however, with the help of this book, you will never again have any trouble playing D11 – or, indeed, any other chords you're likely to be faced with!

2. All keys are covered here, except A♯. You will come across this key so rarely – if at all – that you only need to remember it's the same note as B♭, and any A♯ chords are played exactly the same way as their B♭ equivalents (e.g. A♯7 = B♭7, etc.).

3. ♭♭ is the sign for double flat, and means the note is to be lowered one tone.
   ⤫ is the sign for double sharp, and means the note is to be raised one tone.

The C Collection

C major - C

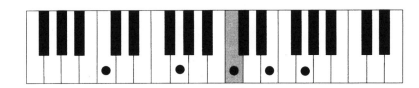

C suspended 4th - Csus or Csus4

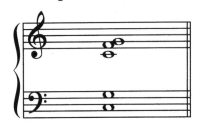

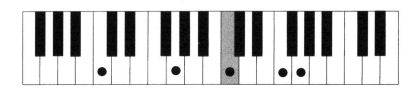

C augmented 5th - C+ or Caug

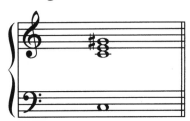

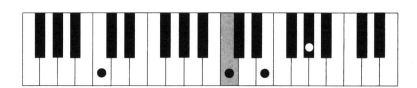

C added 6th - C6

The C Collection

C major 7th - Cmaj7

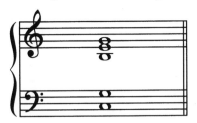

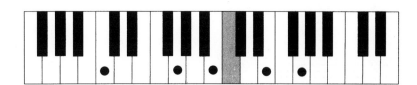

C dominant 7th - C7

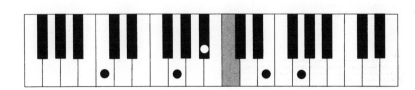

C dominant 7th with suspended 4th - C7sus or C7sus4

C dominant 7th with flattened 5th - C7(♭5)

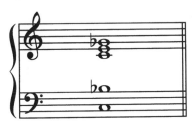

The C Collection

C dominant 7th with augmented 5th - C7+ or C7aug

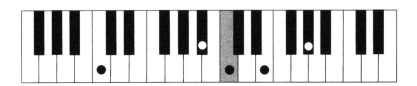

C dominant 7th with flattened 9th - C7(♭9)

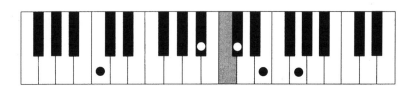

C dominant 7th with sharpened 9th - C7(♯9)

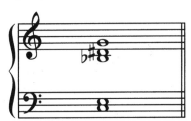

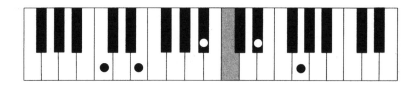

C added 9th - Cadd9

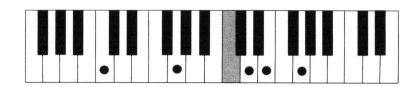

The C Collection

C dominant 9th - C9

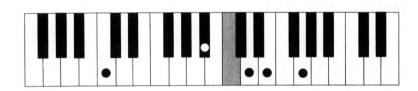

C dominant 9th with suspended 4th - C9sus or C9sus4

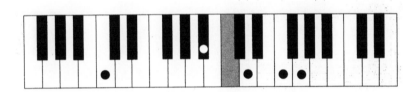

C dominant 9th with augmented 5th - C9+ or C9aug

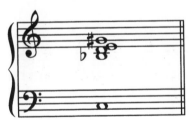

C dominant 11th - C11

The C Collection

C dominant 13th - C13

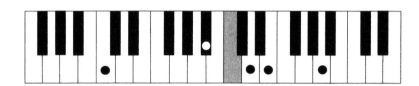

C minor - Cm

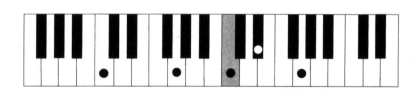

C diminished - C ° or Cdim

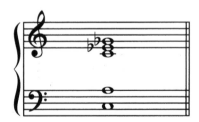

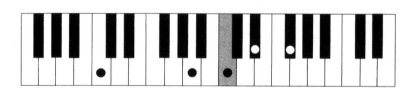

C minor added 6th - Cm6

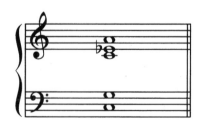

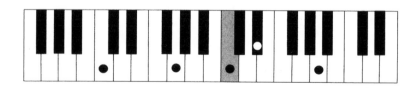

The C Collection

C minor 7th - Cm7

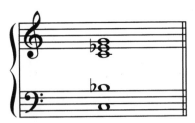
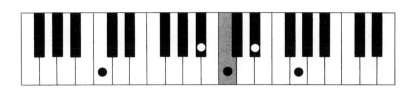

C minor 7th with flattened 5th - Cm7(♭5)

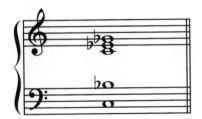
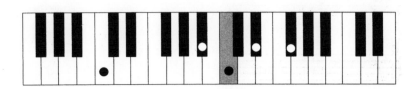

C minor added major 7th - Cm(maj7)

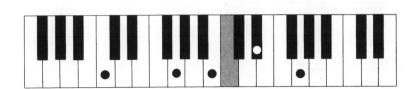

C minor 9th - Cm9

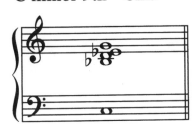

The C♯ Collection

C♯ major - C♯

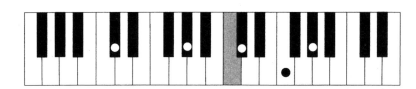

C♯ suspended 4th - C♯sus or C♯sus4

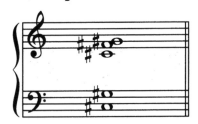

C♯ augmented 5th - C♯+ or C♯aug

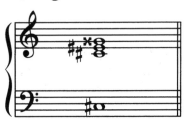

C♯ added 6th - C♯6

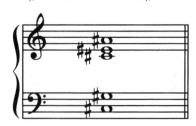
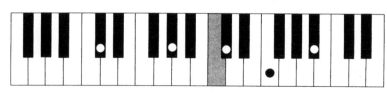

C♯ and D♭ are the same note spelled in different ways, depending on the key you are in.
For this reason, C♯ and D♭ chords are grouped together on facing pages.

The D♭ Collection

D♭ major - D♭

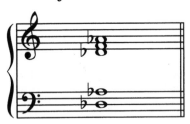

D♭ suspended 4th - D♭sus or D♭sus4

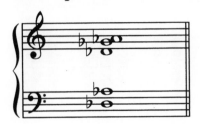

D♭ augmented 5th - D♭+ or D♭aug

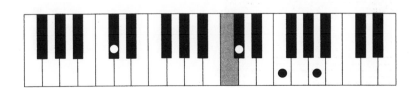

D♭ added 6th - D♭6

The C♯ Collection

C♯ major 7th - C♯maj7

 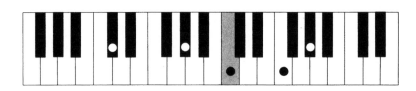

C♯ dominant 7th - C♯7

 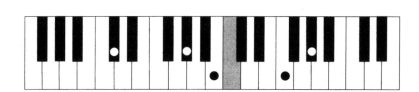

C♯ dominant 7th with suspended 4th - C♯7sus or C♯7sus4

 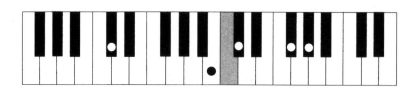

C♯ dominant 7th with flattened 5th - C♯7(♭5)

 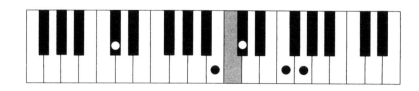

The D♭ Collection

Db major 7th - Dbmaj7

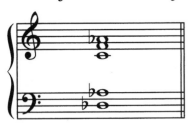

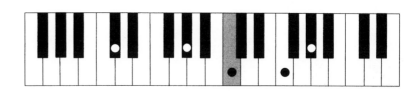

Db dominant 7th - Db7

Db dominant 7th with suspended 4th - Db7sus or Db7sus4

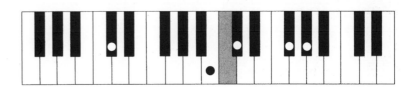

Db dominant 7th with flattened 5th - Db7(b5)

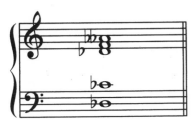

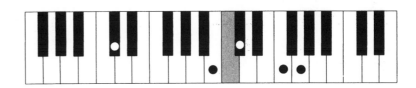

The C♯ Collection

C♯ dominant 7th with augmented 5th - C♯7+ or C♯7aug

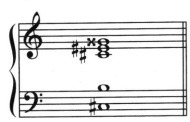 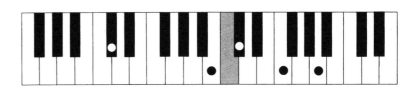

C♯ dominant 7th with flattened 9th - C♯7(♭9)

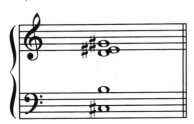 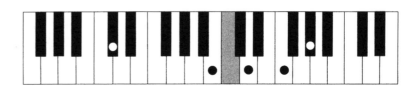

C♯ dominant 7th with sharpened 9th - C♯7(♯9)

C♯ added 9th - C♯add9

 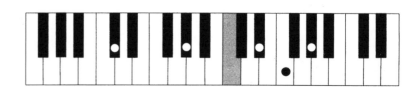

The D♭ Collection

D♭ dominant 7th with augmented 5th - D♭7+ or D♭7aug

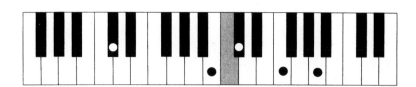

D♭ dominant 7th with flattened 9th - D♭7(♭9)

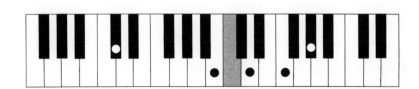

D♭ dominant 7th with sharpened 9th - D♭7(♯9)

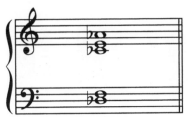

D♭ added 9th - D♭add9

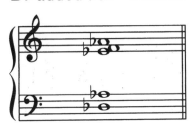

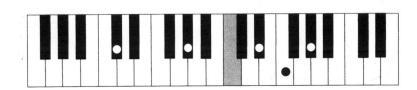

The C♯ Collection

C♯ dominant 9th - C♯9

C♯ dominant 9th with suspended 4th - C♯9sus or C♯9sus4

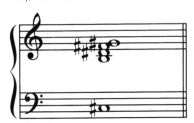

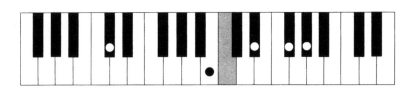

C♯ dominant 9th with augmented 5th - C♯9+ or C♯9aug

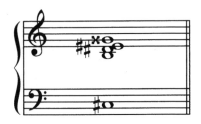

C♯ dominant 11th - C♯11

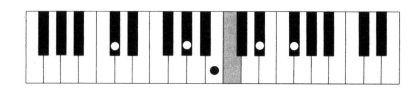

The D♭ Collection

Db dominant 9th - D♭9

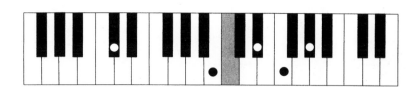

Db dominant 9th with suspended 4th - D♭9sus or D♭9sus4

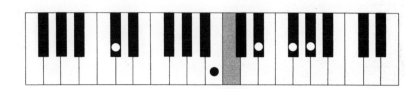

Db dominant 9th with augmented 5th - D♭9+ or D♭9aug

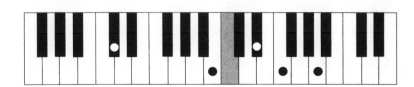

Db dominant 11th - D♭11

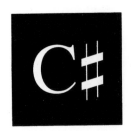

The C♯ Collection

C♯ dominant 13th - C♯13

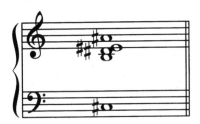

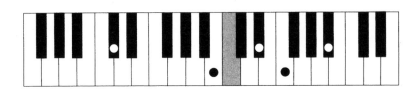

C♯ minor - C♯m

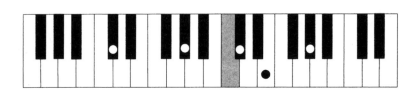

C♯ diminished - C♯° or C♯dim

C♯ minor added 6th - C♯m6

The D♭ Collection

D♭ dominant 13th - D♭13

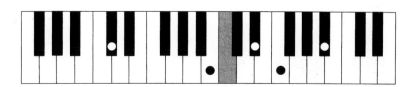

D♭ minor - D♭m

D♭ diminished - D♭° or D♭dim

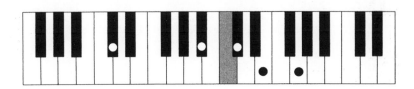

D♭ minor added 6th - D♭m6

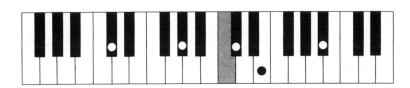

The C♯ Collection

C♯ minor 7th - C♯m7

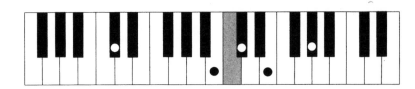

C♯ minor 7th with flattened 5th - C♯m7(♭5)

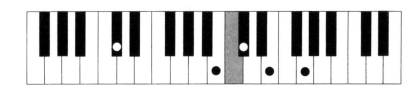

C♯ minor added major 7th - C♯m(maj7)

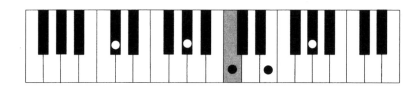

C♯ minor 9th - C♯m9

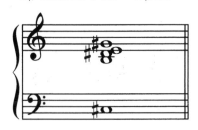

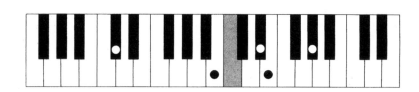

The D♭ Collection

D♭ minor 7th - D♭m7

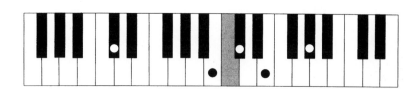

D♭ minor 7th with flattened 5th - D♭m7(♭5)

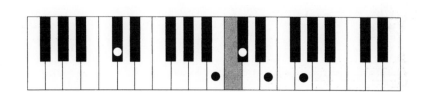

D♭ minor added major 7th - D♭m(maj7)

D♭ minor 9th - D♭m9

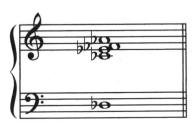

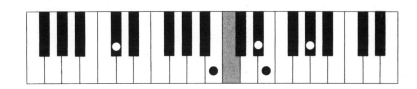

The D Collection

D major - D

D suspended 4th - Dsus or Dsus4

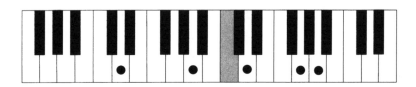

D augmented 5th - D+ or Daug

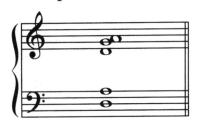

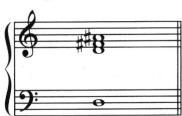

D added 6th - D6

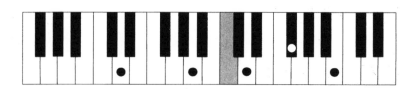

The D Collection

D major 7th - Dmaj7

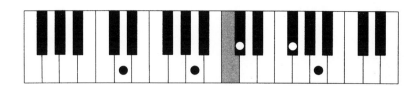

D dominant 7th - D7

D dominant 7th with suspended 4th - D7sus or D7sus4

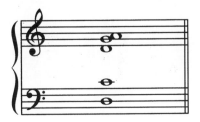

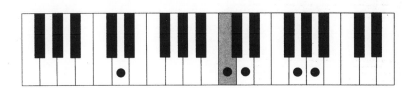

D dominant 7th with flattened 5th - D7(♭5)

The D Collection

D dominant 7th with augmented 5th - D7+ or D7aug

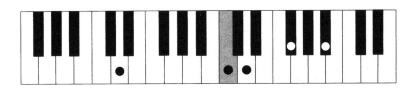

D dominant 7th with flattened 9th - D7(♭9)

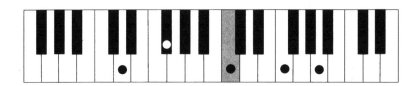

D dominant 7th with sharpened 9th - D7(♯9)

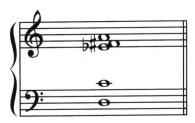

D added 9th - Dadd9

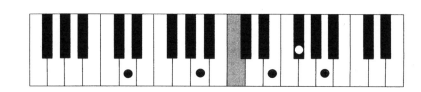

The D Collection

D dominant 9th - D9

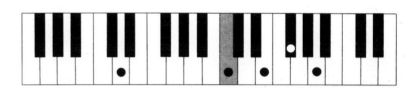

D dominant 9th with suspended 4th - D9sus or D9sus4

D dominant 9th with augmented 5th - D9+ or D9aug

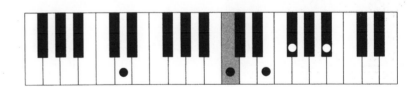

D dominant 11th - D11

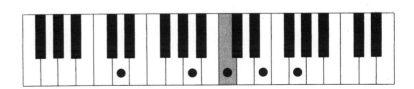

The D Collection

D dominant 13th - D13

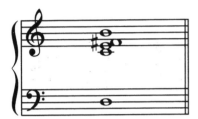

D minor - Dm

D diminished - D° or Ddim

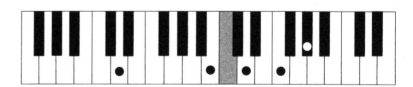

D minor added 6th - Dm6

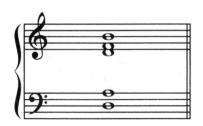

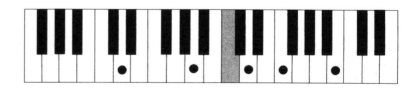

The D Collection

D minor 7th - Dm7

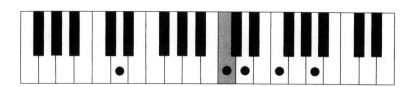

D minor 7th with flattened 5th - Dm7(♭5)

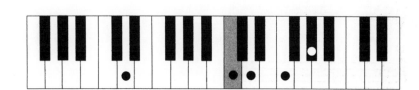

D minor added major 7th - Dm(maj7)

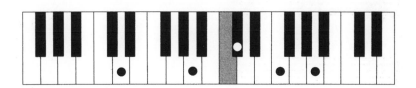

D minor 9th - Dm9

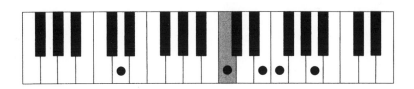

The D♯ Collection

D♯ major - D♯

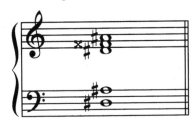

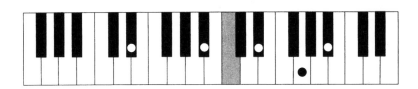

D♯ suspended 4th - D♯sus or D♯sus4

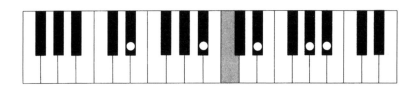

D♯ augmented 5th - D♯+ or D♯aug

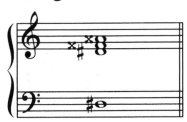

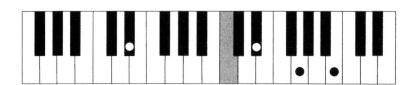

D♯ added 6th - D♯6

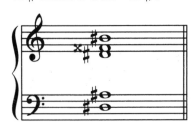

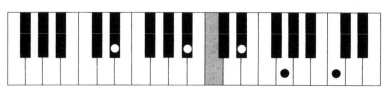

D♯ and E♭ are the same note spelled in different ways, depending on the key you are in.
For this reason, D♯ and E♭ chords are grouped together on facing pages.

The E♭ Collection

E♭ major - E♭

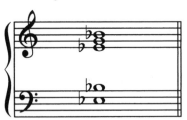
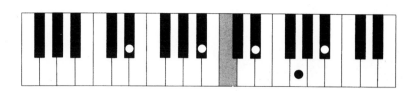

E♭ suspended 4th - E♭sus or E♭sus4

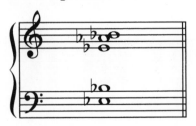

E♭ augmented 5th - E♭+ or E♭aug

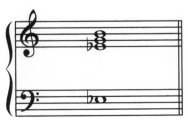

E♭ added 6th - E♭6

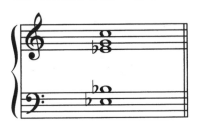

The D♯ Collection

D♯ major 7th - D♯maj7

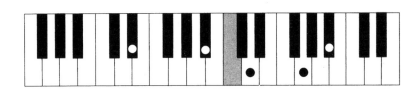

D♯ dominant 7th - D♯7

D♯ dominant 7th with suspended 4th - D♯7sus or D♯7sus4

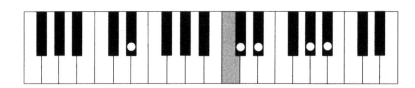

D♯ dominant 7th with flattened 5th - D♯7(♭5)

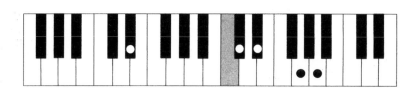

The E♭ Collection

E♭ major 7th - E♭maj7

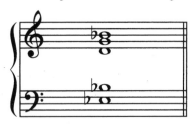

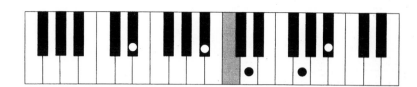

E♭ dominant 7th - E♭7

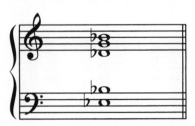

E♭ dominant 7th with suspended 4th - E♭7sus or E♭7sus4

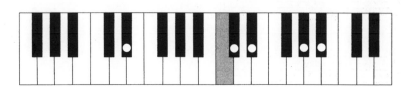

E♭ dominant 7th with flattened 5th - E♭7(♭5)

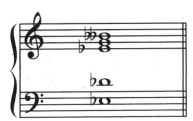

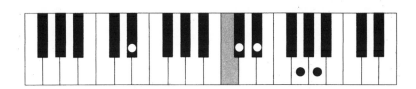

The D♯ Collection

D♯ dominant 7th with augmented 5th - D♯7+ or D♯7aug

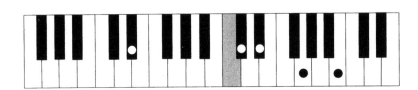

D♯ dominant 7th with flattened 9th - D♯7(♭9)

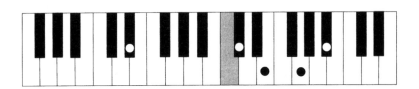

D♯ dominant 7th with sharpened 9th - D♯7(♯9)

D♯ added 9th - D♯add9

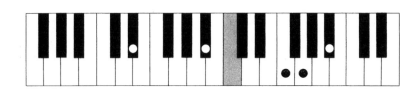

The E♭ Collection

E♭ dominant 7th with augmented 5th - E♭7+ or E♭7aug

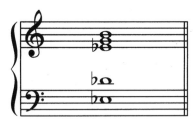
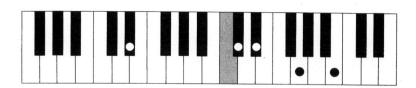

E♭ dominant 7th with flattened 9th - E♭7(♭9)

E♭ dominant 7th with sharpened 9th - E♭7(♯9)

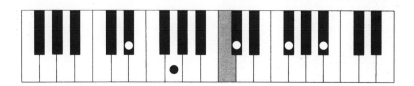

E♭ added 9th - E♭add9

The D♯ Collection

D♯ dominant 9th - D♯9

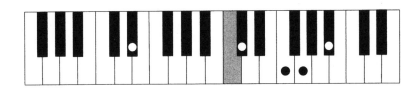

D♯ dominant 9th with suspended 4th - D♯9sus or D♯9sus4

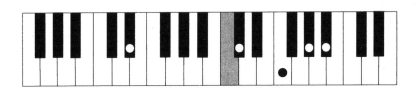

D♯ dominant 9th with augmented 5th - D♯9+ or D♯9aug

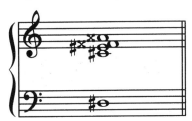

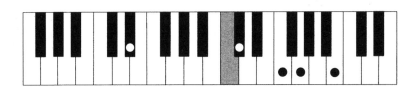

D♯ dominant 11th - D♯11

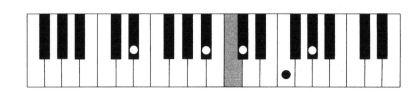

The E♭ Collection

E♭ dominant 9th - E♭9

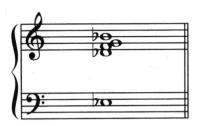

E♭ dominant 9th with suspended 4th - E♭9sus or E♭9sus4

E♭ dominant 9th with augmented 5th - E♭9+ or E♭9aug

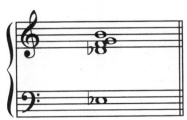
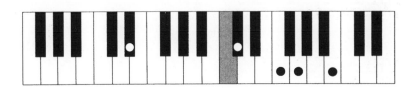

E♭ dominant 11th - E♭11

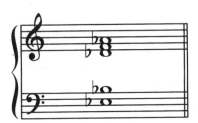
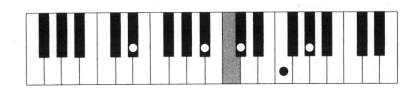

The D♯ Collection

D♯ dominant 13th - D♯13

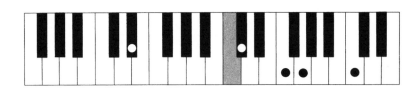

D♯ minor - D♯m

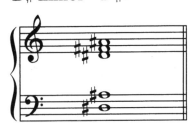

D♯ diminished - D♯° or D♯dim

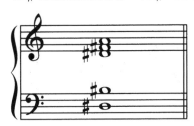
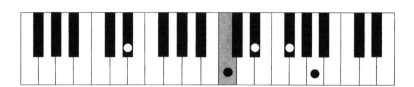

D♯ minor added 6th - D♯m6

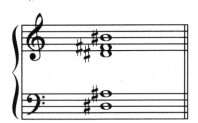
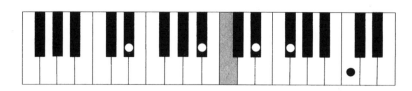

The E♭ Collection

E♭ dominant 13th - E♭13

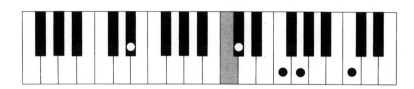

E♭ minor - E♭m

E♭ diminished - E♭° or E♭dim

E♭ minor added 6th - E♭m6

The D♯ Collection

D♯ minor 7th - D♯m7

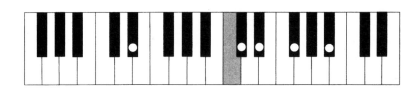

D♯ minor 7th with flattened 5th - D♯m7(♭5)

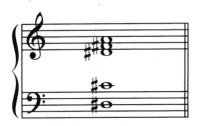

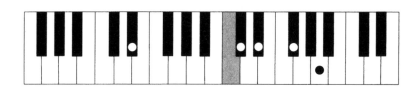

D♯ minor added major 7th - D♯m(maj7)

D♯ minor 9th - D♯m9

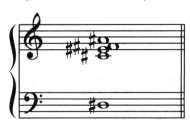

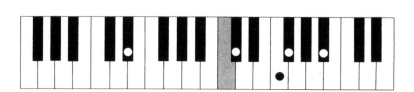

The E♭ Collection

E♭ minor 7th - E♭m7

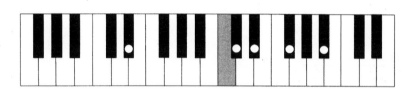

E♭ minor 7th with flattened 5th - E♭m7(♭5)

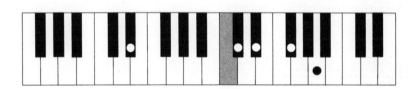

E♭ minor added major 7th - E♭m(maj7)

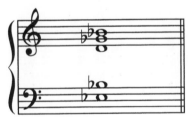

E♭ minor 9th - E♭m9

The E Collection

E major - E

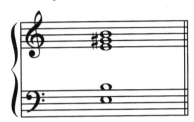

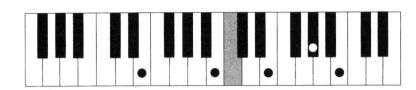

E suspended 4th - Esus or Esus4

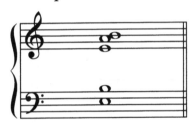

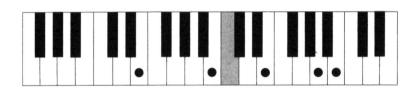

E augmented 5th - E+ or Eaug

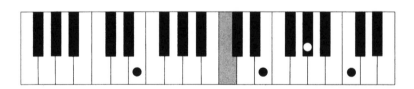

E added 6th - E6

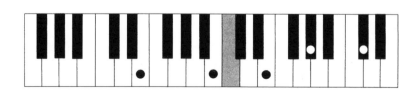

The E Collection

E major 7th - Emaj7

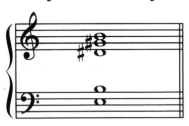

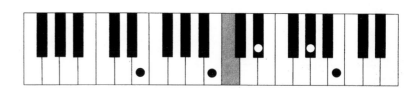

E dominant 7th - E7

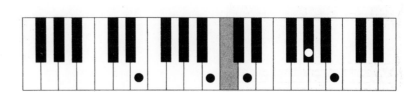

E dominant 7th with suspended 4th - E7sus or E7sus4

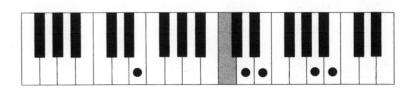

E dominant 7th with flattened 5th - E7(♭5)

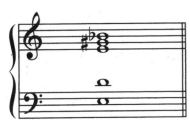

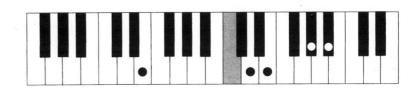

The E Collection

E dominant 7th with augmented 5th - E7+ or E7aug

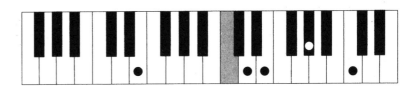

E dominant 7th with flattened 9th - E7(♭9)

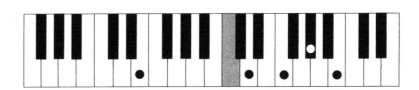

E dominant 7th with sharpened 9th - E7(♯9)

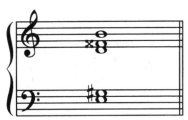

E added 9th - Eadd9

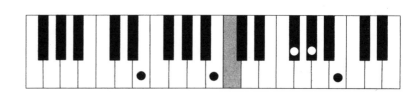

The E Collection

E dominant 9th - E9

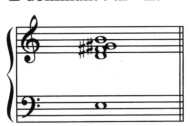

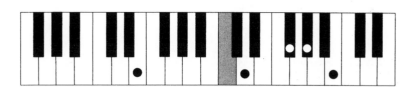

E dominant 9th with suspended 4th - E9sus or E9sus4

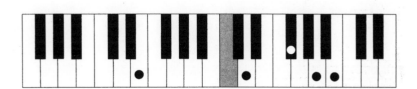

E dominant 9th with augmented 5th - E9+ or E9aug

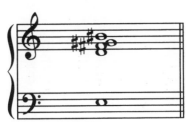

E dominant 11th - E11

The E Collection

E dominant 13th - E13

E minor - Em

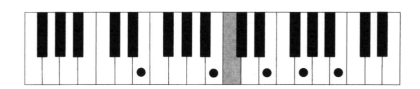

E diminished - E° or Edim

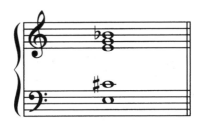

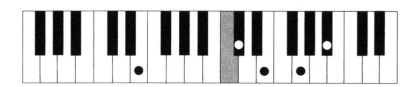

E minor added 6th - Em6

The E Collection

E minor 7th - Em7

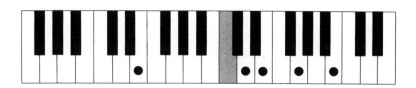

E minor 7th with flattened 5th - Em7(♭5)

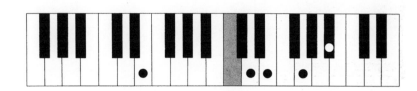

E minor added major 7th - Em(maj7)

E minor 9th - Em9

The F Collection

F major - F

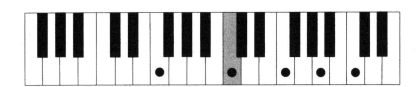

F suspended 4th - Fsus or Fsus4

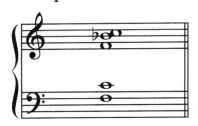

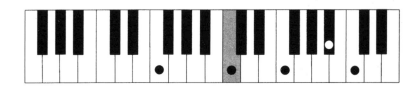

F augmented 5th - F+ or Faug

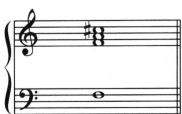

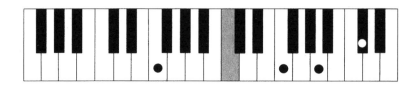

F added 6th - F6

The F Collection

F major 7th - Fmaj7

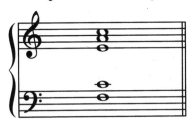

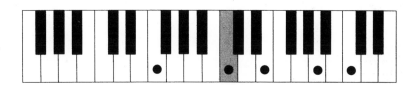

F dominant 7th - F7

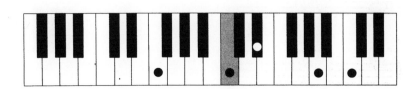

F dominant 7th with suspended 4th - F7sus or F7sus4

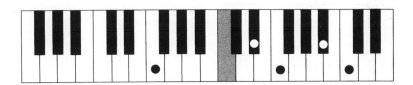

F dominant 7th with flattened 5th - F7(♭5)

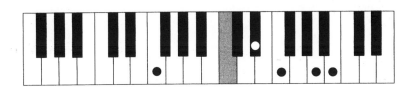

The F Collection

F dominant 7th with augmented 5th - F7+ or F7aug

F dominant 7th with flattened 9th - F7(♭9)

F dominant 7th with sharpened 9th - F7(♯9)

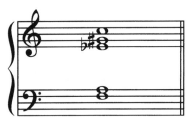
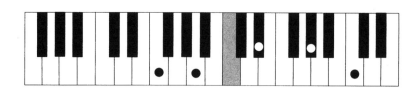

F added 9th - Fadd9

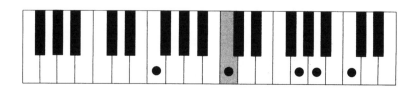

The F Collection

F dominant 9th - F9

F dominant 9th with suspended 4th - F9sus or F9sus4

 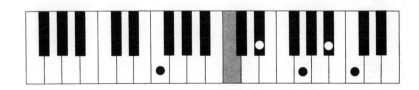

F dominant 9th with augmented 5th - F9+ or F9aug

 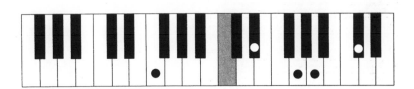

F dominant 11th - F11

The F Collection

F dominant 13th - F13

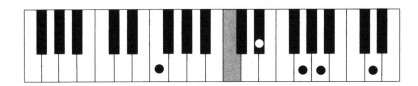

F minor - Fm

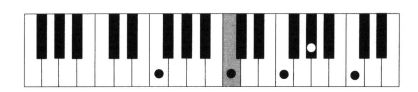

F diminished - F° or Fdim

F minor added 6th - Fm6

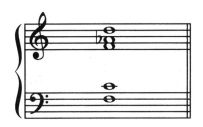

The F Collection

F minor 7th - Fm7

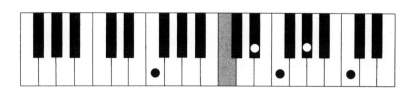

F minor 7th with flattened 5th - Fm7(♭5)

F minor added major 7th - Fm(maj7)

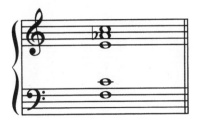

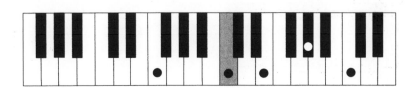

F minor 9th - Fm9

The F♯ Collection

F♯ major - F♯

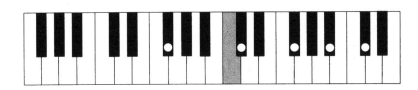

F♯ suspended 4th - F♯sus or F♯sus4

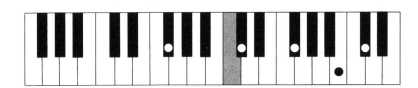

F♯ augmented 5th - F♯+ or F♯aug

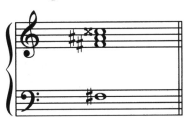

F♯ added 6th - F♯6

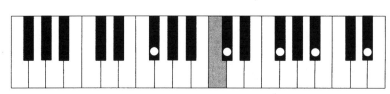

F♯ and G♭ are the same note spelled in different ways, depending on the key you are in.
For this reason, F♯ and G♭ chords are grouped together on facing pages.

The G♭ Collection

G♭ major - G♭

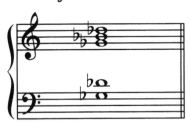
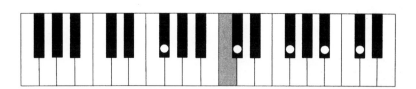

G♭ suspended 4th - G♭sus or G♭sus4

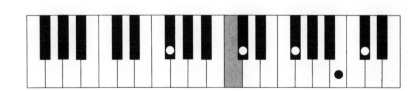

G♭ augmented 5th - G♭+ or G♭aug

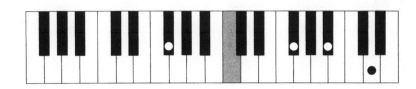

G♭ added 6th - G♭6

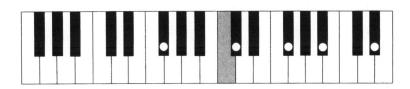

The F♯ Collection

F♯ major 7th - F♯maj7

F♯ dominant 7th - F♯7

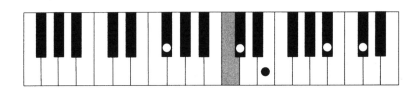

F♯ dominant 7th with suspended 4th - F♯7sus or F♯7sus4

F♯ dominant 7th with flattened 5th - F♯7(♭5)

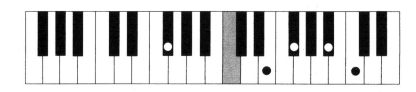

The G♭ Collection

Gb major 7th - Gbmaj7

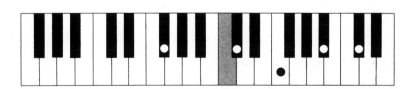

Gb dominant 7th - Gb7

Gb dominant 7th with suspended 4th - Gb7sus or Gb7sus4

Gb dominant 7th with flattened 5th - Gb7(b5)

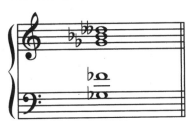

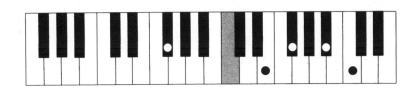

The F♯ Collection

F♯ dominant 7th with augmented 5th - F♯7+ or F♯7aug

F♯ dominant 7th with flattened 9th - F♯7(♭9)

 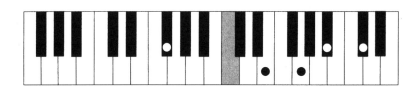

F♯ dominant 7th with sharpened 9th - F♯7(♯9)

 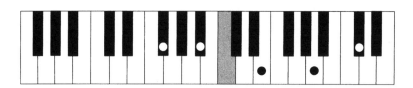

F♯ added 9th - F♯add9

The G♭ Collection

G♭ dominant 7th with augmented 5th - G♭7+ or G♭7aug

G♭ dominant 7th with flattened 9th - G♭7(♭9)

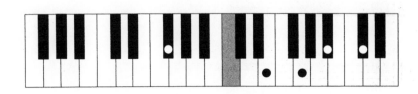

G♭ dominant 7th with sharpened 9th - G♭7(♯9)

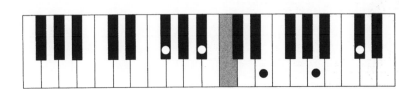

G♭ added 9th - G♭add9

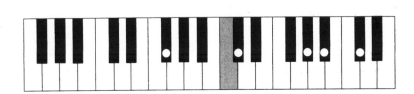

The F♯ Collection

F♯ dominant 9th - F♯9

 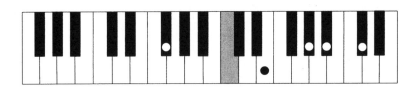

F♯ dominant 9th with suspended 4th - F♯9sus or F♯9sus4

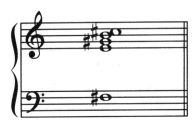 

F♯ dominant 9th with augmented 5th - F♯9+ or F♯9aug

 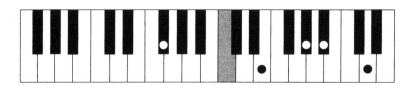

F♯ dominant 11th - F♯11

 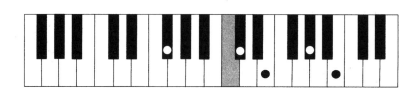

The G♭ Collection

G♭ dominant 9th - G♭9

G♭ dominant 9th with suspended 4th - G♭9sus or G♭9sus4

G♭ dominant 9th with augmented 5th - G♭9+ or G♭9aug

 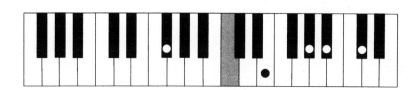

G♭ dominant 11th - G♭11

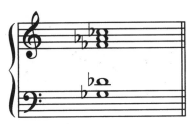 

The F♯ Collection

F♯ dominant 13th - F♯13

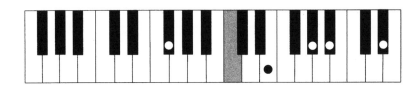

F♯ minor - F♯m

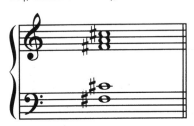

F♯ diminished - F♯° or F♯dim

F♯ minor added 6th - F♯m6

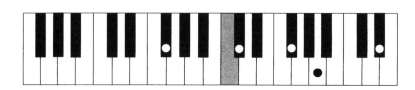

The G♭ Collection

G♭ dominant 13th - G♭13

 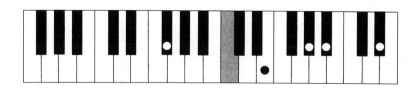

G♭ minor - G♭m

G♭ diminished - G♭° or G♭dim

 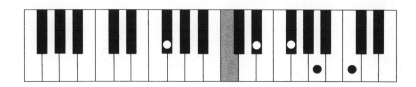

G♭ minor added 6th - G♭m6

 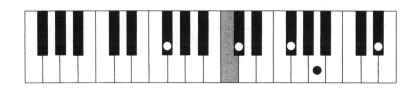

The F♯ Collection

F♯ minor 7th - F♯m7

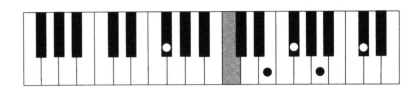

F♯ minor 7th with flattened 5th - F♯m7(♭5)

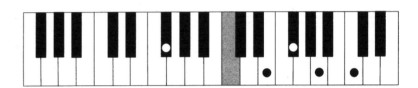

F♯ minor added major 7th - F♯m(maj7)

F♯ minor 9th - F♯m9

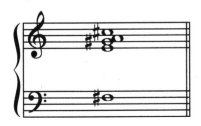

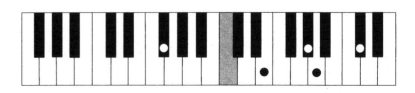

The G♭ Collection

G♭ minor 7th - G♭m7

G♭ minor 7th with flattened 5th - G♭m7(♭5)

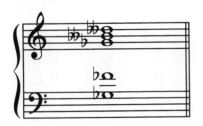

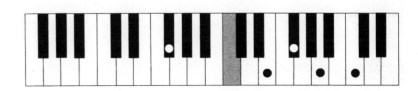

G♭ minor added major 7th - G♭m(maj7)

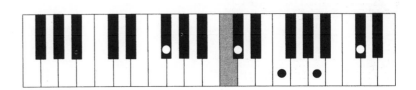

G♭ minor 9th - G♭m9

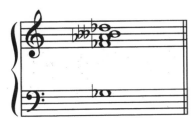

The G Collection

G major - G

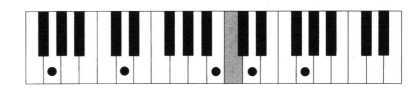

G suspended 4th - Gsus or Gsus4

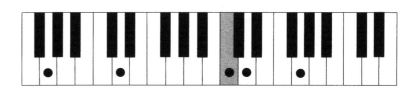

G augmented 5th - G+ or Gaug

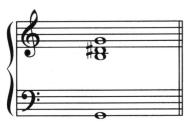

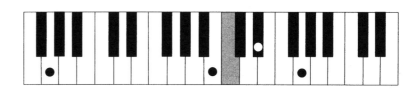

G added 6th - G6

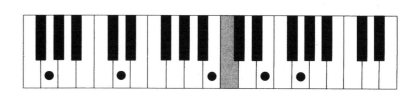

The G Collection

G major 7th - Gmaj7

 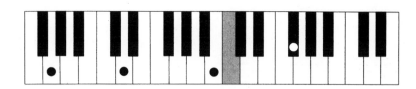

G dominant 7th - G7

 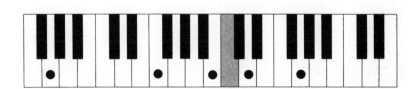

G dominant 7th with suspended 4th - G7sus or G7sus4

 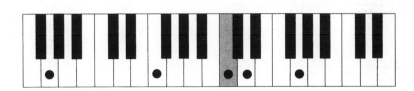

G dominant 7th with flattened 5th - G7(♭5)

 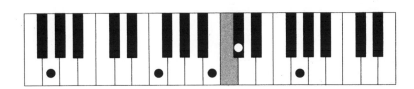

The G Collection

G dominant 7th with augmented 5th - G7+ or G7aug

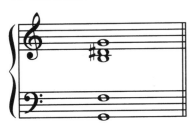

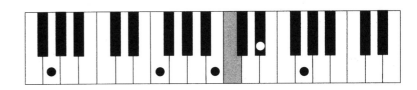

G dominant 7th with flattened 9th - G7(♭9)

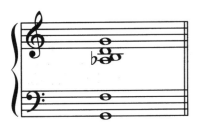

G dominant 7th with sharpened 9th - G7(♯9)

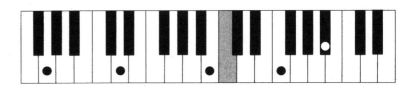

G added 9th - Gadd9

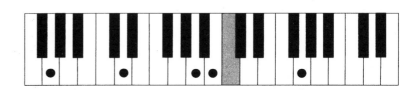

The G Collection

G dominant 9th - G9

G dominant 9th with suspended 4th - G9sus or G9sus4

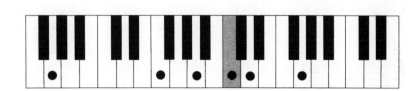

G dominant 9th with augmented 5th - G9+ or G9aug

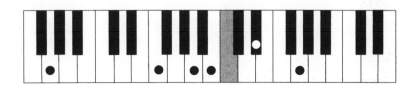

G dominant 11th - G11

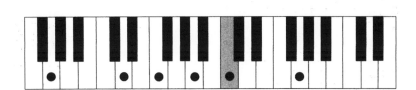

The G Collection

G dominant 13th - G13

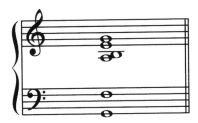

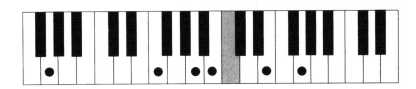

G minor - Gm

G diminished - G° or Gdim

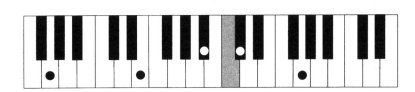

G minor added 6th - Gm6

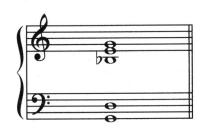

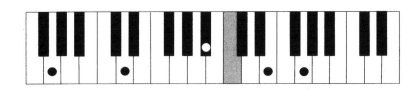

The G Collection

G minor 7th - Gm7

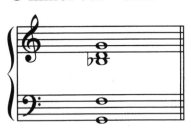
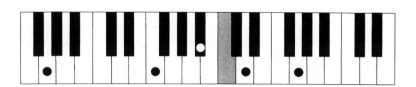

G minor 7th with flattened 5th - Gm7(♭5)

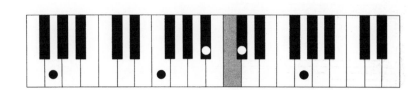

G minor added major 7th - Gm(maj7)

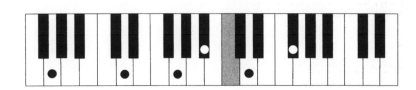

G minor 9th - Gm9

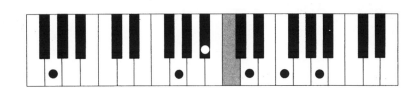

The G♯ Collection

G♯ major - G♯

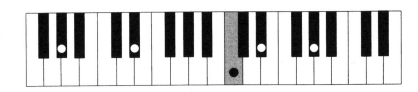

G♯ suspended 4th - G♯sus or G♯sus4

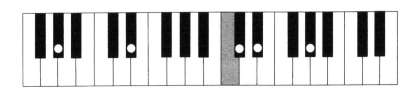

G♯ augmented 5th - G♯+ or G♯aug

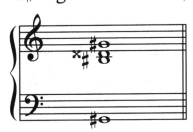

G♯ added 6th - G♯6

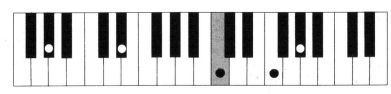

G♯ and A♭ are the same note spelled in different ways, depending on the key you are in.
For this reason, G♯ and A♭ chords are grouped together on facing pages.

The A♭ Collection

A♭ major - A♭

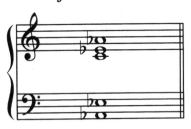 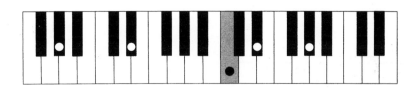

A♭ suspended 4th - A♭sus or A♭sus4

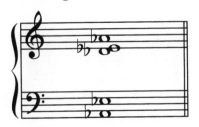 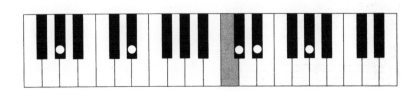

A♭ augmented 5th - A♭+ or A♭aug

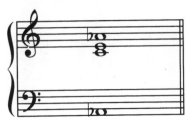 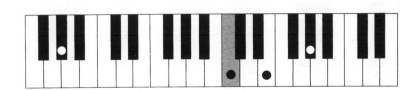

A♭ added 6th - A♭6

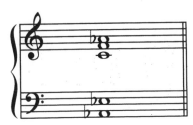 

The G♯ Collection

G♯ major 7th - G♯maj7

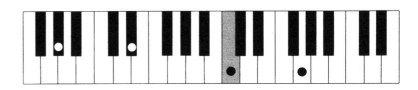

G♯ dominant 7th - G♯7

G♯ dominant 7th with suspended 4th - G♯7sus or G♯7sus4

G♯ dominant 7th with flattened 5th - G♯7(♭5)

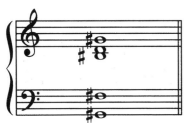
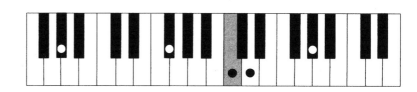

The A♭ Collection

A♭ major 7th - A♭maj7

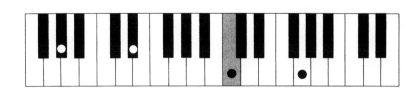

A♭ dominant 7th - A♭7

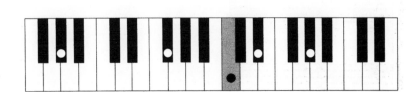

A♭ dominant 7th with suspended 4th - A♭7sus or A♭7sus4

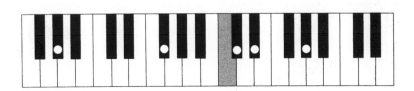

A♭ dominant 7th with flattened 5th - A♭7(♭5)

The G♯ Collection

G♯ dominant 7th with augmented 5th - G♯7+ or G♯7aug

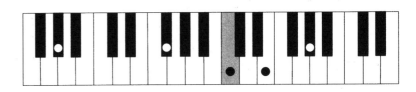

G♯ dominant 7th with flattened 9th - G♯7(♭9)

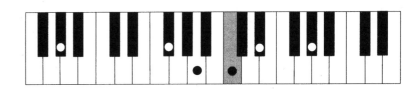

G♯ dominant 7th with sharpened 9th - G♯7(♯9)

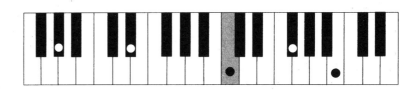

G♯ added 9th - G♯add9

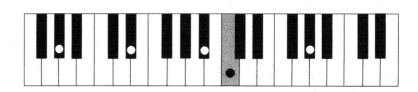

The A♭ Collection

A♭ dominant 7th with augmented 5th - A♭7+ or A♭7aug

A♭ dominant 7th with flattened 9th - A♭7(♭9)

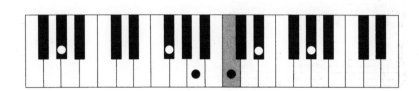

A♭ dominant 7th with sharpened 9th - A♭7(#9)

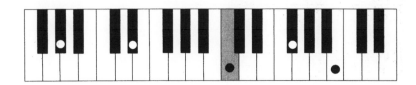

A♭ added 9th - A♭add9

The G♯ Collection

G♯ dominant 9th - G♯9

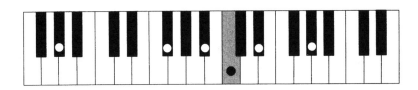

G♯ dominant 9th with suspended 4th - G♯9sus or G♯9sus4

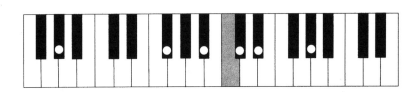

G♯ dominant 9th with augmented 5th - G♯9+ or G♯9aug

G♯ dominant 11th - G♯11

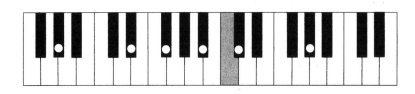

The A♭ Collection

A♭ dominant 9th - A♭9

A♭ dominant 9th with suspended 4th - A♭9sus or A♭9sus4

A♭ dominant 9th with augmented 5th - A♭9+ or A♭9aug

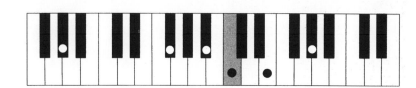

A♭ dominant 11th - A♭11

The G♯ Collection

G♯ dominant 13th - G♯13

G♯ minor - G♯m

G♯ diminished - G♯° or G♯dim

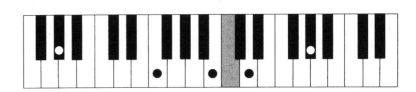

G♯ minor added 6th - G♯m6

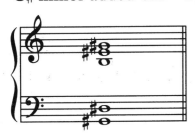

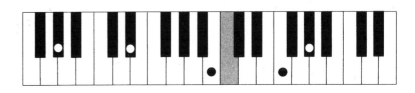

The A♭ Collection

A♭ dominant 13th - A♭13

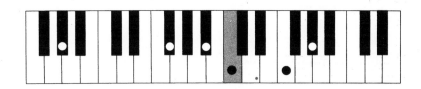

A♭ minor - A♭m

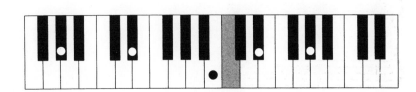

A♭ diminished - A♭° or A♭dim

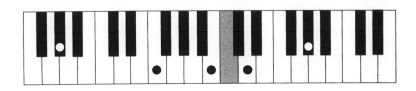

A♭ minor added 6th - A♭m6

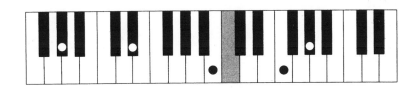

The G♯ Collection

G♯ minor 7th - G♯m7

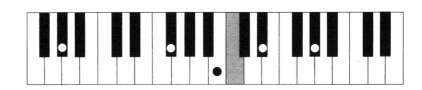

G♯ minor 7th with flattened 5th - G♯m7(♭5)

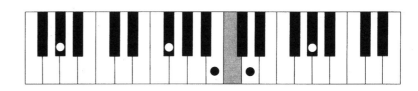

G♯ minor added major 7th - G♯m(maj7)

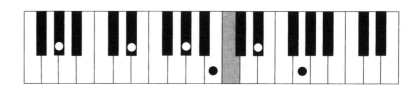

G♯ minor 9th - G♯m9

The A♭ Collection

A♭ minor 7th - A♭m7

A♭ minor 7th with flattened 5th - A♭m7(♭5)

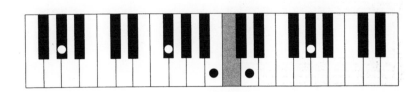

A♭ minor added major 7th - A♭m(maj7)

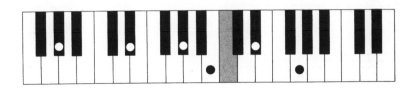

A♭ minor 9th - A♭m9

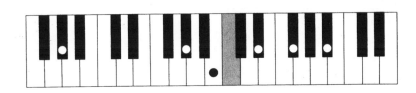

The A Collection

A major - A

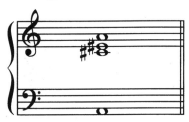

A suspended 4th - Asus or Asus4

A augmented 5th - A+ or Aaug

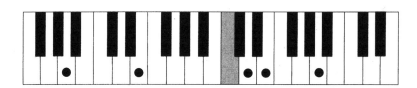

A added 6th - A6

The A Collection

A major 7th - Amaj7

A dominant 7th - A7

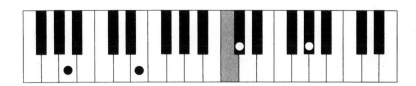

A dominant 7th with suspended 4th - A7sus or A7sus4

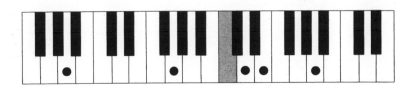

A dominant 7th with flattened 5th - A7(♭5)

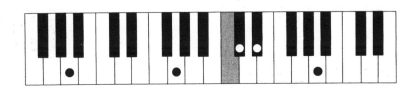

The A Collection

A dominant 7th with augmented 5th - A7+ or A7aug

A dominant 7th with flattened 9th - A7(♭9)

 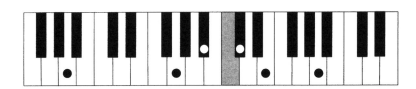

A dominant 7th with sharpened 9th - A7(♯9)

 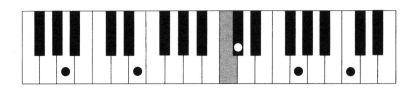

A added 9th - Aadd9

The A Collection

A dominant 9th - A9

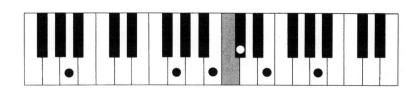

A dominant 9th with suspended 4th - A9sus or A9sus4

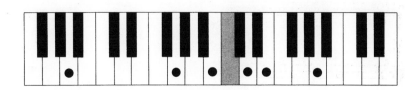

A dominant 9th with augmented 5th - A9+ or A9aug

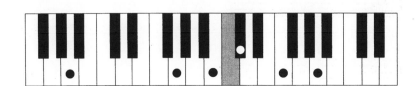

A dominant 11th - A11

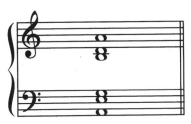

The A Collection

A dominant 13th - A13

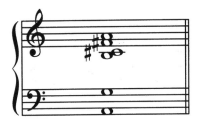
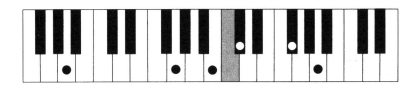

A minor - Am

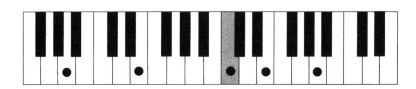

A diminished - A° or Adim

A minor added 6th - Am6

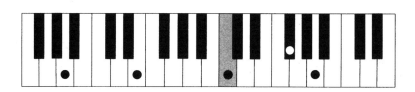

The A Collection

A minor 7th - Am7

A minor 7th with flattened 5th - Am7(♭5)

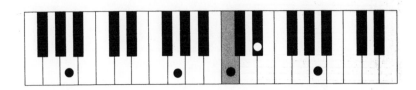

A minor added major 7th - Am(maj7)

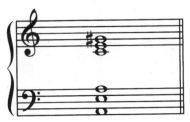

A minor 9th - Am9

The B♭ Collection

Bb major - Bb

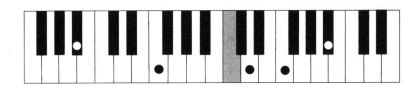

Bb suspended 4th - Bbsus or Bbsus4

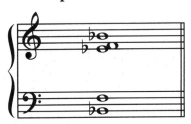

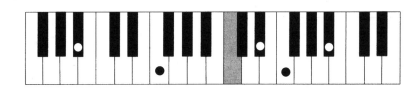

Bb augmented 5th - Bb+ or Bbaug

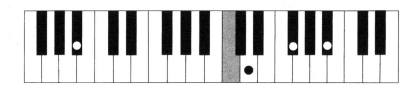

Bb added 6th - Bb6

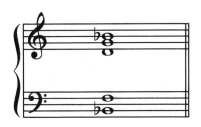

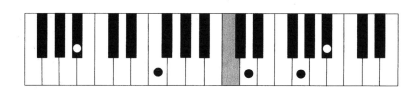

The B♭ Collection

B♭ major 7th - B♭maj7

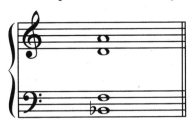

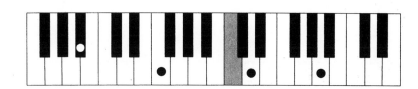

B♭ dominant 7th - B♭7

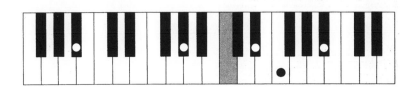

B♭ dominant 7th with suspended 4th - B♭7sus or B♭7sus4

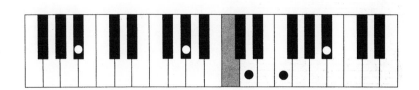

B♭ dominant 7th with flattened 5th - B♭7(♭5)

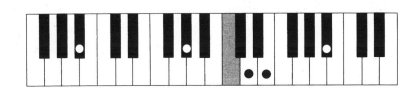

The B♭ Collection

Bb dominant 7th with augmented 5th - Bb7+ or Bbaug

Bb dominant 7th with flattened 9th - Bb7(b9)

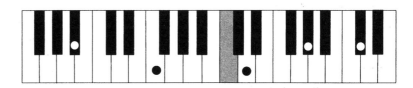

Bb dominant 7th with sharpened 9th - Bb7(♯9)

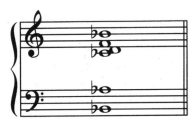

Bb added 9th - Bbadd9

The B♭ Collection

B♭ dominant 9th - B♭9

B♭ dominant 9th with suspended 4th - B♭9sus B♭9sus4

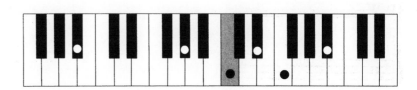

B♭ dominant 9th with augmented 5th - B♭9+ or B♭9aug

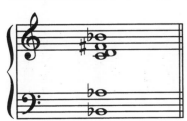

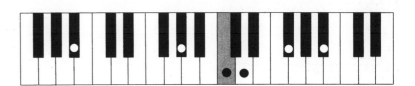

B♭ dominant 11th - B♭11

The B♭ Collection

B♭ dominant 13th - B♭13

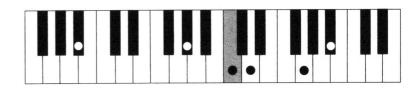

B♭ minor - B♭m

B♭ diminished - B♭° or B♭dim

B♭ minor added 6th - B♭m6

The B♭ Collection

B♭ minor 7th - B♭m7

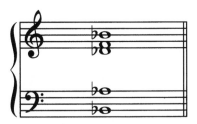

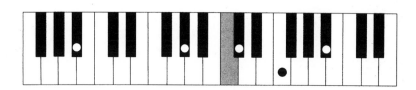

B♭ minor 7th with flattened 5th - B♭m7(♭5)

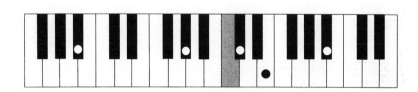

B♭ minor added major 7th - B♭m(maj7)

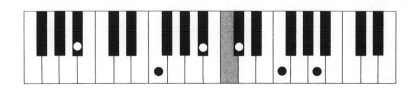

B♭ minor 9th - B♭m9

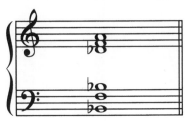

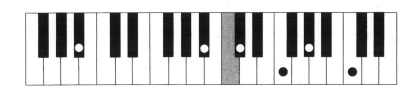

The B Collection

B major - B

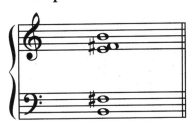

B suspended 4th - Bsus or Bsus4

B augmented 5th - B+ or Baug

B added 6th - B6

The B Collection

B major 7th - Bmaj7

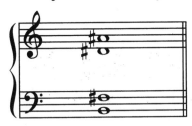
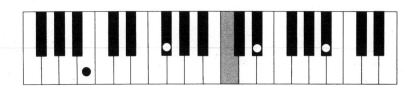

B dominant 7th - B7

B dominant 7th with suspended 4th - B7sus or B7sus4

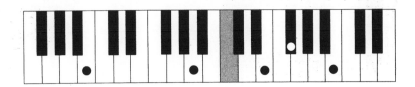

B dominant 7th with flattened 5th - B7(♭5)

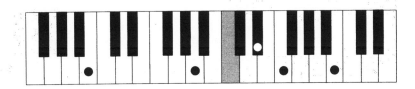

The B Collection

B dominant 7th with augmented 5th - B7+ or B7aug

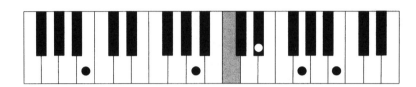

B dominant 7th with flattened 9th - B7(♭9)

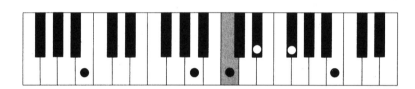

B dominant 7th with sharpened 9th - B7(♯9)

B added 9th - Badd9

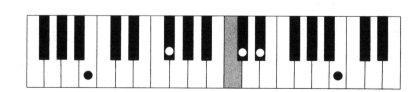

The B Collection

B dominant 9th - B9

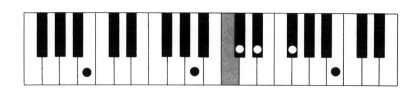

B dominant 9th with suspended 4th - B9sus or B9sus4

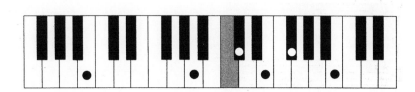

B dominant 9th with augmented 5th - B9+ or B9aug

B dominant 11th - B11

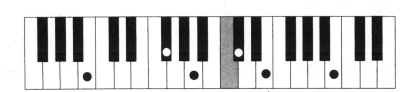

The B Collection

B dominant 13th - B13

B minor - Bm

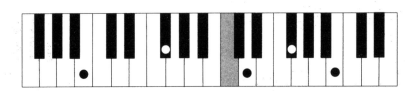

B diminished - B° or Bdim

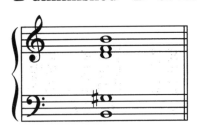

B minor added 6th - Bm6

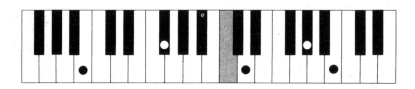

The B Collection

B minor 7th - Bm7

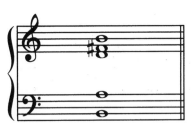
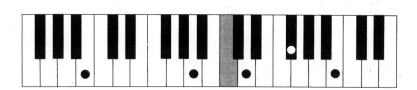

B minor 7th with flattened 5th - Bm7(♭5)

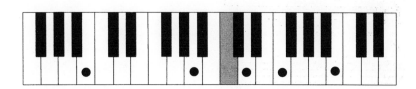

B minor added major 7th - Bm(maj7)

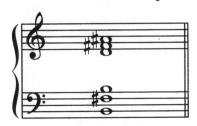

B minor 9th - Bm9

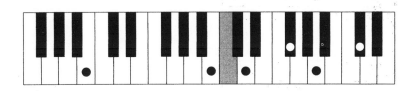

Your Own Collection

Why not use the charts below to notate your favourite chord voicings?

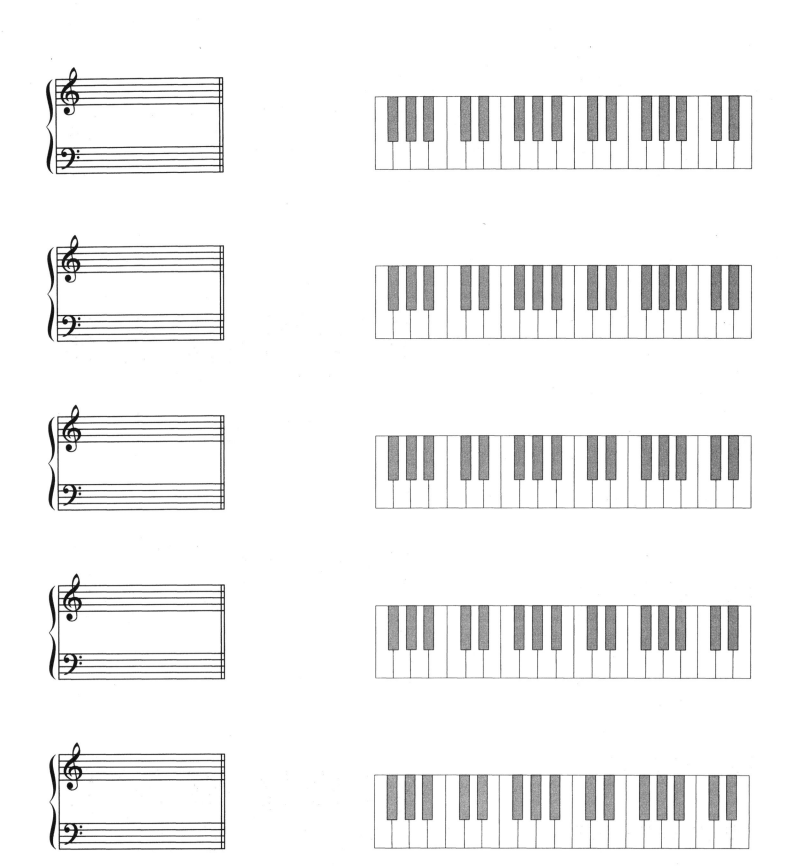

Your Own Collection

Why not use the charts below to notate your favourite chord voicings?

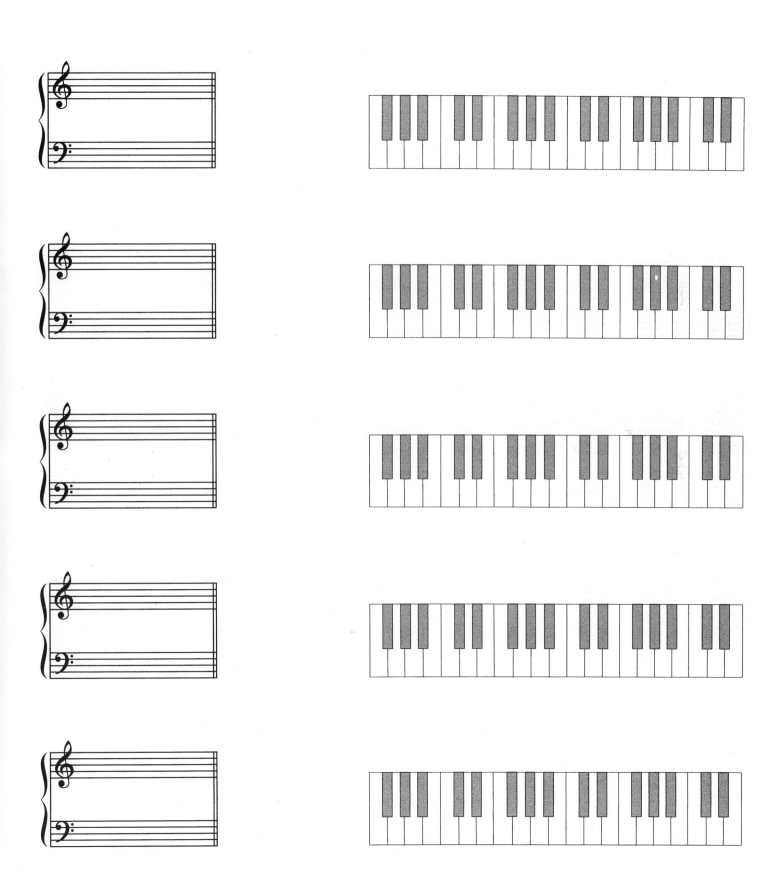

Your Own Collection

Why not use the charts below to notate your favourite chord voicings?

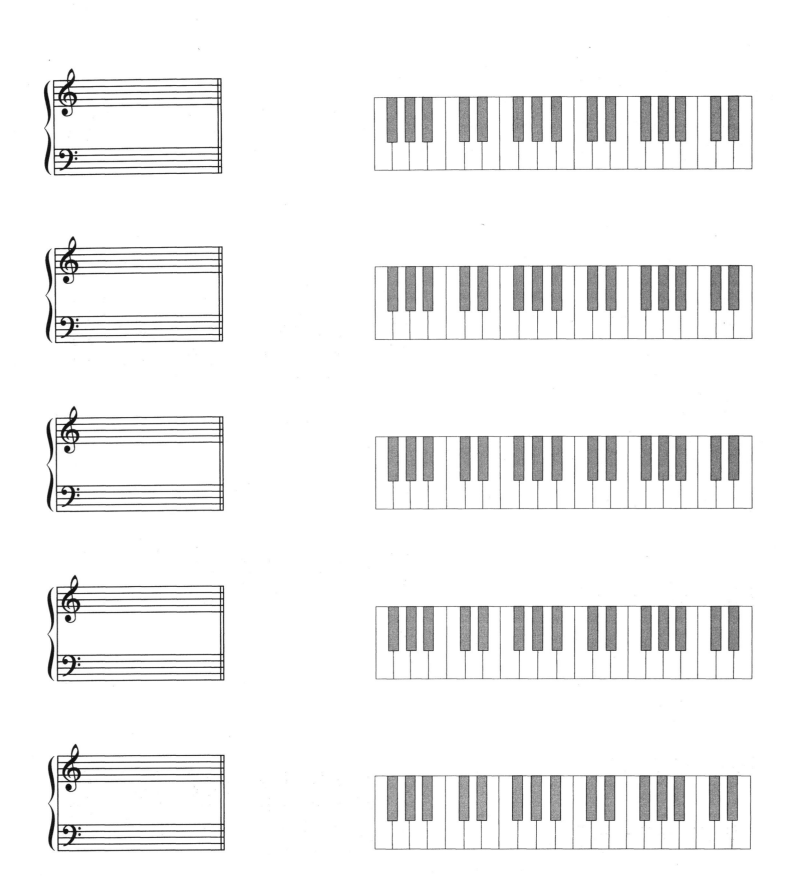

Your Own Collection

Why not use the charts below to notate your favourite chord voicings?

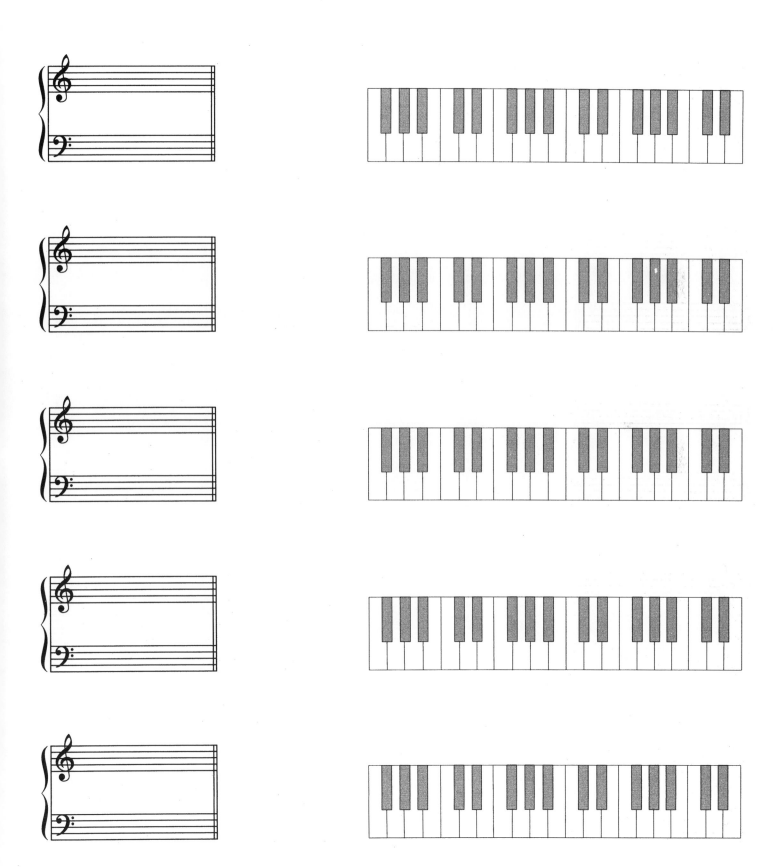

Your Own Collection

Why not use the charts below to notate your favourite chord voicings?

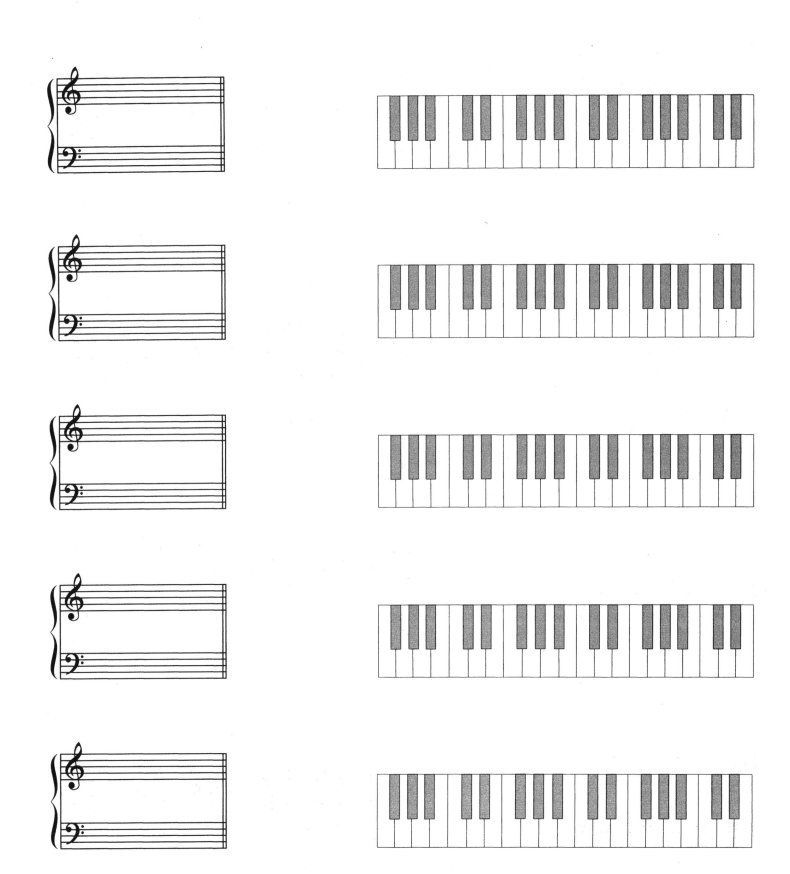

Your Own Collection

Why not use the charts below to notate your favourite chord voicings?

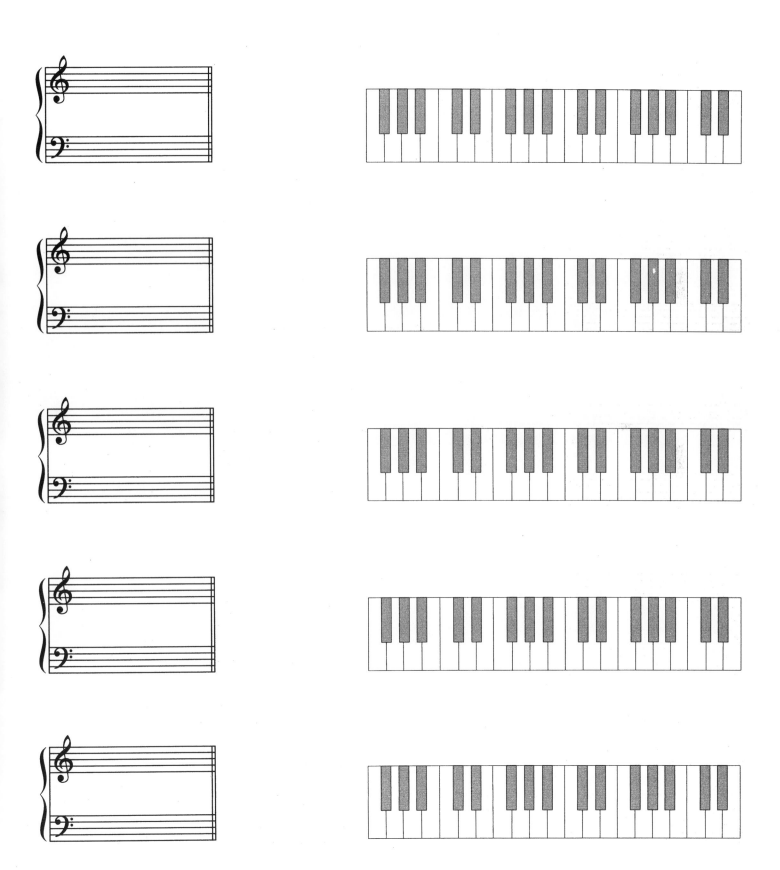

Index Of Chords

(in ascending order within the scale of C)

Printed in Great Britain   5/09 (169836)

Bringing you the words and the music

All the latest music in print... rock & pop plus jazz, blues, country, classical and the best in West End show scores.

- Books to match your favourite CDs.

- Book-and-CD titles with high quality backing tracks for you to play along to. Now you can play guitar or piano with your favourite artist... or simply sing along!

- Audition songbooks with CD backing tracks for both male and female singers for all those with stars in their eyes.

- Can't read music? No problem, you can still play all the hits with our wide range of chord songbooks.

- Check out our range of instrumental tutorial titles, taking you from novice to expert in no time at all!

- Musical show scores include *The Phantom Of The Opera*, *Les Misérables*, *Mamma Mia* and many more hit productions.

- DVD master classes featuring the techniques of top artists.